CATECHISM
of
MENTAL PRAYER

D0945849

CATECHISM
of
MENTAL PRAYER

by

Very Rev. Joseph Simler
Superior General of The Society of Mary

"The devil knows that he has lost the soul that perseveringly practices mental prayer."
—St. Teresa of Avila

TAN Books
An Imprint of Saint Benedict Press, LLC
Charlotte, North Carolina

Nihil Obstat: Aloysius Schratz, S.M.
                  Censor Deputatus

Imprimatur: ✠ Henricus Moeller
                  Archiepiscopus
                  Cincinnatensis

Library of Congress Catalog Card No.: 84-51901

ISBN: 978-0-89555-256-3

Printed and bound in the United States of America.

TAN Books
An Imprint of Saint Benedict Press, LLC
Charlotte, North Carolina
2012

PREFACE

This little "Catechism" is a substantial summary of the *Guide of the Man of Good Will in the Exercise of Mental Prayer* by the same author.

It is published with the view of aiding especially the young in the proper understanding and practice of mental prayer. It treats the subject with so much clearness and simplicity that any person of good will cannot but study it with profit.

Although the book is intended alike for general and private use, its present form and arrangement will render it particularly serviceable as a textbook in novitiates, preparatory seminaries, and other institutions where young persons are initiated into the practices of a religious life.

May God abundantly bless this little work, and grant that it may serve to render the practice of mental prayer both profitable and easy. May the august Queen of Heaven, the patroness of devout souls, look down with approval upon the efforts of all who shall study its pages: may she herself teach them the art of praying well, that they may gradually be brought to an ever more perfect knowledge and love both of herself and of her divine Son.

CONTENTS

Preface v
I General Ideas 1
  1. Nature of Mental Prayer 1
  2. Necessity and Excellence of
       Mental Prayer 3
  3. Facility of Mental Prayer 6
II Preparation for Mental Prayer 9
  1. Remote or Habitual Preparation .. 9
  2. Proximate Preparation 11
  3. Immediate Preparation 13
III Body of Mental Prayer 16
  1. Principal Acts of the
       Body of Mental Prayer 16
  2. Considerations 18
  3. Affections 22
  4. Resolutions 26
  5. The Order and Connection of
       These Acts 28
IV Conclusion of Mental Prayer 30
V Examination of Mental Prayer 32
VI Mixed Mental Prayer 34
VII Difficulties Encountered
    in Mental Prayer 38
  1. Distractions 38
  2. Aridity 41

   3. Illusions 43

Supplement 45

  Acts of the Preparation 45

  Acts of the Body of Mental Prayer 49

  Acts of the Conclusion 50

A Choice of Subjects for Meditation 52

A Choice of Spiritual Bouquets 54

Questions for the Examination of
  Mental Prayer 61

Practical Remarks 63

A Final Reminder 67

CATECHISM
of
MENTAL PRAYER

CHAPTER I

GENERAL IDEAS

§ 1. Nature of Mental Prayer

1. What is prayer?
Prayer is an elevation of our soul toward God to render Him our homage.

2. How does the soul elevate itself toward God?
The soul elevates itself toward God by thinking of Him, loving Him, and conversing with Him.

3. What kinds of homage should we render to God?
We should render to God four kinds of homage: We should adore Him, beg His pardon for our sins, thank Him for His benefits, and petition His graces.

4. How many kinds of prayer are there?
There are two kinds of prayer: vocal prayer and mental prayer.

5. What is meant by vocal prayer?

By vocal prayer is meant every prayer performed by means of a given formula.

6. Why are such prayers called vocal prayers?

They are so called because ordinarily the voice is used in reciting them.

7. What is meant by mental prayer?

By mental prayer is meant every prayer performed without aid of any particular formula.

8. Why is this kind of prayer called mental prayer?

It is so called because it is made by the mind, generally without any articulation of words.

9. What is mental prayer ordinarily called?

It is ordinarily called meditation.

10. In what does mental prayer essentially consist?

Mental prayer essentially consists in thinking of God or of holy things, with the intention, at least virtual, of rendering Him our homage. Thus every pious thought, every pious desire, is a mental prayer.

11. Give a more complete definition of mental prayer.

Mental prayer is a pious communication of

the soul with God by means of considerations,
affections, and resolutions. Its object is to make
us know, love, and serve God better, and to
promote the knowledge of ourselves and the
faithful discharge of our duties. In practice,
therefore, it is the art of becoming better.

§ 2. NECESSITY AND EXCELLENCE OF MENTAL PRAYER

12. Is mental prayer necessary?
Mental prayer, in its essence, is necessary
for every Christian who wishes to be saved.

13. Demonstrate this necessity.
1. Every Christian is obliged to pray; it is
impossible for him to pray well without reflecting on what he says, consequently, without
meditating.
2. Without meditation, he does not know
his wants, and therefore does not think of
praying. Thus, meditation is as necessary for
him as is prayer in general.

14. How else can you prove this necessity?
Without meditation, everything is done by
routine; and, by degrees, routine leads to
thoughtlessness, spiritual blindness, and insen-
sibility. Hence, the Holy Ghost says: "With des-

olation is all the land made desolate; because there is none that considereth in the heart." (*Jer.* 12:11).

15. Is it a duty of state for a religious to practice mental prayer?

Yes: 1. Because without mental prayer he cannot advance toward perfection, for which he ought unceasingly to strive.

2. Because without mental prayer he will be much exposed to losing his vocation, as is proved by experience. Therefore, the founders of religious orders and the masters of the spiritual life have made this holy exercise a duty of state for religious persons.

16. Has the religious who is devoted to an active life any special reason for applying himself to mental prayer?

Yes: 1. Because mental prayer is the only means which can efficaciously preserve him from the spirit of the world, and keep up in him the spirit of faith.

2. Because the salvation of souls is above all the work of grace, and grace is obtained principally by prayer.

3. Because Our Lord, Who came on earth to save mankind, devoted far more time to prayer than to preaching.

4. Because the Apostles freed themselves from all other cares, in order to devote themselves exclusively to prayer and to the ministry of the word. (*Acts* 6:4).

5. Because those evangelical laborers who gained the most souls for God distinguished themselves by their application to mental prayer.

17. Is mental prayer an exercise of any particular excellence?

Yes, mental prayer is most excellent, not merely by reason of its necessity, but also on account of its advantages, and because it is most honorable for us.

18. Name some of the advantages of mental prayer.

By the light and strength it imparts to us, mental prayer:

1. Keeps sin far from us and saves us from Hell.

2. Preserves us from lukewarmness, or cures us of it.

3. Is the common source of all virtues. It is thus the shortest way of arriving at perfection, and the most efficacious means of persevering in our vocation.

19. Why is mental prayer such a great honor for us?

Because in mental prayer we are admitted to the audience, not of a prince, of an earthly ruler, but to that of God Himself.

§ 3. FACILITY OF MENTAL PRAYER

20. Is mental prayer easy?

Yes, mental prayer is easy, whether it be considered on the part of God, or on the part of man.

21. Show that meditation is easy when considered on the part of God.

Since meditation is necessary for everybody, God must make its practice easy, because only easy things can be performed by all men.

22. Show that mental prayer is easy when considered on the part of man.

To make mental prayer means to recall to mind, with the help of grace, some good thoughts, to make in all simplicity acts of faith, hope, and charity, of confidence and humility, of repentance and firm purpose of amendment, of petition, etc. Who would affirm that this is something difficult?

23. Does mental prayer not also offer some difficulties?

Mental prayer does offer some difficulties, as does every work, and every struggle of virtue against vice.

24. Whence come these difficulties?

They come:

1. From the devil, who endeavors to keep us from this holy exercise.

2. From spiritual sloth, which deters us from efforts which must be renewed, as it were, every day.

3. From discouragement, which we experience in finding ourselves always combating numerous faults and defects, combined with a false persuasion that we cannot correct ourselves of them.

4. From our sins, which pull our mind, heart and will away from God and from prayer. It is not possible to persevere in mental prayer and at the same time to persist in sin, especially not in mortal sin.

25. What then is necessary to make mental prayer well?

It is necessary to have a sincere will, i.e., we must earnestly apply ourselves to mental prayer, and constantly beg this grace of God.

26. By what signs can we know that we make mental prayer well?

The tree is known by its fruits; thus we can know what our meditation is worth by its results.

27. What results does a good meditation produce?

It produces a greater fidelity to the duties of one's state, especially a greater love for humility, the mother of all virtues, for obedience, their guardian, and for charity, their queen.

CHAPTER II

PREPARATION FOR MENTAL PRAYER

§ 1. REMOTE OR HABITUAL PREPARATION

28. How is mental prayer divided?

Mental prayer is divided into three parts:

1. The preparation.
2. The body of mental prayer.
3. The conclusion.

29. How can you justify this division?

Mental prayer is rightly compared to a divine audience: there are certain things to be done and observed in every audience. It is necessary:

1. Before the audience, to prepare for it.
2. During the audience, to employ the time thereof in a proper manner.
3. To bring it to a suitable conclusion.

30. How many kinds of preparation are there?

There are three kinds of preparation: the

remote or habitual, the proximate, and the immediate.

31. In what does the habitual preparation for mental prayer consist?

The habitual preparation consists in removing the obstacles in our daily life that prevent us from meditating well, thus disposing ourselves favorably for this holy exercise.

32. What are the chief obstacles that prevent us from performing mental prayer well?

Dissipation and faults against silence, attachment to sin, and slavery to the senses and passions.

33. What means should be taken to remove these obstacles?

The following:

1. Recollection and silence.

2. Purity of heart, which consists in abstaining from all sin committed with full deliberation.

3. Exterior and interior mortification.

34. What are the principal acts of the remote preparation that favor mental prayer?

The habitual remembrance of the presence of God, purity of intention, and frequent recourse to ejaculatory prayers.

§ 2. PROXIMATE PREPARATION

35. In what does the proximate preparation consist?

The proximate preparation consists principally:

1 . In being recollected at the approach of meditation.

2. In foreseeing the subject of mental prayer, the principal considerations, and the fruit that we wish to derive from it.

36. Is the proximate preparation very necessary?

Yes, it is very necessary for two reasons:

1. Because we should be wanting in respect to God were we to appear before Him without knowing the subject of the interview we intend to have.

2. Because, without this preparation, we should be exposed to being lost in the wanderings of our mind.

37. How should the subject of mental prayer be chosen?

The subject of mental prayer should be chosen in accordance with the needs of our soul, the attractions of grace, and the advice of our spiritual director.

38. Are there not certain subjects on which it is useful to meditate repeatedly?

Yes, it is useful to meditate repeatedly on the great truths of salvation, particularly on the last things of man, on the life and Passion of Our Lord, and on the virtues and glories of the Most Blessed Virgin.

39. Is it useful to meditate repeatedly on the same subject?

Yes, it is useful to meditate repeatedly on those subjects which impress us profoundly, and which inspire us with strong resolutions.

40. Is it, then, not necessary to like the subject that is read in the community?

Not absolutely; when the subject that is read in the community is not fitting, we may choose another: in this case it is generally of advantage to take a subject already meditated upon.

41. When is the choice of the subject ordinarily made?

The choice of the subject for the morning meditation is ordinarily made after the night prayers; for the evening meditation it is made during some free moments of the day, during a visit to the Most Blessed Sacrament, or at the spiritual reading. The important thing is that each one have a determined time to make this choice.

42. What else does the proximate preparation comprise?

The proximate preparation comprises also exactness as to the hour and place of meditation.

§ 3. Immediate Preparation

43. What does the immediate preparation comprise?

The immediate preparation, which may be called the introduction to the divine audience, comprises:

1. The invocation to the Holy Ghost, to the Blessed Virgin, and to our Guardian Angel, who acts as usher.

2. An act of faith in the presence of God and of union with Our Lord.

3. Other acts derived from this act of faith, such as acts of humility, confidence, contrition, etc.

44. Is the act of faith in the presence of God very important?

Yes, it is the most important act of the immediate preparation; by neglecting it we should expose ourselves to performing our meditation badly.

45. Is this act of faith very difficult?

No, because to make it well, nothing else is necessary than to recall to mind the reality; for God is present everywhere. No effort of the imagination is required. This act of faith becomes especially easy in the presence of the Blessed Sacrament.

46. Is this act of faith always made in the same manner?

No, it may vary according to the attributes we consider in God, according to the state of our soul, and according to the end we propose to ourselves in mental prayer.

47. In reference to what four attributes may we consider God in mental prayer?

We may consider God:

1. As our Creator, in order to adore Him with profound humility.

2. As our Savior and Judge, to ask pardon for our offenses.

3. As our Benefactor, to thank Him.

4. Above all, as our Father, to invoke Him with an entirely filial confidence.

48. Is it necessary to make all the above mentioned acts at every meditation?

No, we may dwell sometimes on one act, sometimes on another, according to the attractions of grace: however, we should never omit the act of faith in the presence of God, nor the acts of adoration, humility, and confidence.

49. Must we always make use of memorized formulas when making the acts?

It is advantageous to do so; but it would be better to produce these acts spontaneously, if possible, and from the bottom of our heart.

50. How long should these acts last?

Ordinarily they should last but a few minutes: however, when the soul feels so inclined, they may be prolonged even to the close of the exercise.

51. What posture should we assume during meditation?

It is proper to kneel when addressing God: but if this posture becomes too fatiguing we may take another, provided it be respectful.

CHAPTER III

BODY OF MENTAL PRAYER

§ 1. PRINCIPAL ACTS OF THE BODY OF MENTAL PRAYER

52. What is the body of mental prayer?

The body of mental prayer is the interview, properly so called, of the soul with God.

53. How is this interview begun?

By summarily recalling to mind the object and end of the audience, i.e., the subject of mental prayer and the fruit we wish to draw from it; these are sometimes called the first and the second prelude.

54. Is it useful to divide the subject into several points?

Yes, we can thus comprehend and retain it better than if it were considered as a whole.

55. Must we adhere strictly to the division proposed in the meditation books?

No, we may advantageously adopt another division which might present itself to our mind as more satisfactory, or which might be better adapted to the fruit we wish to draw from the meditation.

56. How long should we dwell on each point?

As long as the soul can occupy itself usefully with it.

57. Must we meditate on all the points?

No, this is not necessary; we may dwell on only one point, if this point suffices to occupy our soul during the entire exercise of meditation.

58. Which faculties of the soul are brought into activity during mental prayer?

All the faculties of our soul may be brought into activity; but it is customary to ascribe all the acts of mental prayer to the intellect, the heart, and the will.

59. How are the acts of these three principal faculties designated?

The acts which are produced during mental prayer by the intellect, the heart, and the will, are respectively termed considerations, affections, and resolutions.

§ 2. CONSIDERATIONS

60. What is meant by considerations?

By considerations are meant pious reflections which the mind, aided by the light of faith, produces during the exercise of mental prayer.

61. What does it mean to meditate in the light of faith?

It means to make the truths of faith the rule of our thoughts, judgments, appreciations, and determinations.

62. Why is it necessary to meditate especially in the light of faith?

For two principal reasons:

1. Because faith alone can instruct us infallibly in the things which are important for us to know.

2. Because the light of faith acts at the same time on the intellect, the heart, and the will.

63. Should we, during meditation, neglect the light of reason?

No, because reason is a natural gift with which God favors us to show us our duty.

64. What is the end and purpose of the considerations?

The end we propose to ourselves in the considerations is to know the subject on which we meditate, to penetrate ourselves vividly with it, and to draw practical conclusions from it.

65. Are the considerations, then, very important?

Yes, they are very important, because they produce in us strong convictions, and consequently prepare the way for good resolutions.

66. Can anybody make considerations?

Yes, because even the least cultivated mind can reflect.

67. Are the considerations always made in the same manner?

No, they are made differently, according as the subject of mental prayer is a truth, such as the doctrine that our eternal destination must be either Heaven or Hell—or a fact, such as Our Lord's death on the cross.

68. How should we proceed when the subject of meditation is a truth?

1. We should direct our attention to the proposed truth.

2. We should endeavor to understand its meaning by reflecting on the words, by distinguishing this truth from others, by estab-

lishing comparisons, by deducing conse-
quences, by grasping the extent, the necessity, and the advantages of the truth.

3. We should endeavor to discover the
lessons which it teaches.

**69. What must we do when the truth
becomes more evident to our mind?**

According as the truth becomes more evident to our mind, we must repeat acts of faith
like the following: "O my God, I believe this
truth, but increase my faith; penetrate me
more deeply with it."

**70. Is it useful to study the proposed truth
also in the lives of Our Lord, of the Blessed
Virgin, and of the Saints?**

Yes, this is very useful, because Our Lord is
the Model of all sanctity, and the Blessed Virgin and the saints are the most faithful copies
of this Divine Model. We may, for instance,
ask ourselves questions like the following:
"How did our Savior, the Blessed Virgin and
the saints think and act in respect to this
truth?" "What difference is there between
their conduct and mine?"

**71. What else must we do in order to ren-
der the proposed truth practical?**

We must examine what our conduct has been in the past with regard to this truth, what it is at present, and what it should be hereafter. Questions like the following may be of use here: "Do I adhere to this teaching?"—"Was it the rule of my appreciations and conduct in the past?"—"Am I at present disposed to take it for the rule of my conduct?"—"What would a lost soul do in this regard if it could come back into life?"—"What would a saint advise me to do?"—"What would I like to have done at the hour of death?"

72. Is it useful to lay special stress on the motives which should induce us to put into practice the maxim or truth on which we meditate?

Yes, this is very useful, because the more deeply we are penetrated with these motives, the more forcibly our will is impelled to adopt energetic resolutions.

73. How should we proceed when the subject of mental prayer is a fact?

1. We should, with our imagination, figure ourselves beholding the scene, place, and persons of the fact, listening to all that is said, and assisting at all that is done.

2. We should endeavor to understand the

meaning of all we have heard and seen with our imagination.

3. We should endeavor to discover the lessons which the fact teaches us.

74. What is the manner of meditating when the subject of mental prayer is a virtue?

A virtue being no more than a truth put into practice, the manner of meditating on a virtue is the same as that of meditating on a truth.

75. What dangers must we avoid while making the considerations?

Principally three:

1. Such an application of the mind as would make of meditation a study rather than a prayer.

2. A search after sublime and purely theoretical considerations.

3. Idleness, be it on account of discouragement, disgust, fatigue, or any other cause.

§ 3. AFFECTIONS

76. What is meant by affections?

By affections are meant the good sentiments which the heart feels during meditation, and which induce the will to make good resolutions.

77. How many kinds of affections are there?
There are two kinds: spontaneous affections and voluntary affections.

78. What are spontaneous affections?
Spontaneous affections are such as present themselves without having been sought after.

79. What are voluntary affections?
Voluntary affections are such as are produced by reflection.

80. Enumerate various kinds of affections.
1. Affections of humility, fear, regret, and gratitude. These generally refer to the past.
2. Affections of fervor, love, and holy desire. These generally refer to the present.
3. Affections of hope, confidence, submission to God's holy will, and good promises. These generally refer to the future.
4. Affections of supplication. These may refer to the past, the present, and the future.

81. What is meant more particularly by supplications?
By supplications are meant ejaculatory prayers and petitions of all kinds which we address to God during meditation.

82. May we address to God supplications on behalf of others?

We not only may, but should do so: on behalf of the Church, the society to which we belong, and those persons whose interest we have at heart, such as the members of our community, our pupils, our parents.

83. Must we endeavor to call forth indiscriminately all kinds of affections?

No, it is advantageous to adhere to those with which God inspires us, to those which relate to our necessities, or which proceed naturally from the subject of the meditation.

84. Can we always produce affections at will during meditation?

Yes, we can, even in dryness and abandonment; for in meditation the affections are ordinary desires, regrets, petitions, and invocations, that is to say, acts in which the will plays the greater part: and man is always master of his will.

85. Should affections have a prominent place in meditation?

Yes, affections, especially those of supplication, should ordinarily occupy a large portion of the time of meditation. Mental prayer is more the work of the heart and will than of the head.

86. Mention an easy means of eliciting affections.

An easy means of eliciting affections consists in having recourse to supplications, and in addressing ourselves to God, to the Blessed Virgin, and to the saints, in the same manner as we would speak to our father, to our mother, or to our friends, if we were in their presence.

87. What should we think of certain sensible attractions which we might sometimes experience during meditation?

Frequently they are graces and encouragements which God gives us as a help to make mental prayer better; but these attractions and consolations do not depend on our will; besides, they are neither necessary nor meritorious in themselves. We can make excellent meditations without experiencing the least consolation. (In this context, the word "sensible" means "of the senses"; the phrase "sensible attractions" refers to tender sentiments.)

88. Should we not even distrust certain sensible affections?

Yes, such are the affections which, pro-

ceeding from an altogether too natural sen-
sibility, do not result in good resolutions.
Affections of this kind easily lead to illusions.

§ 4. RESOLUTIONS

89. What is meant by resolutions?

By resolutions are meant firm purposes of
the will to avoid sin and practice virtue.

90. Are resolutions very important?

Yes, because they constitute the principal
fruit of mental prayer; without them this exercise would, for the most part, remain sterile.

**91. How can we succeed in making good
resolutions?**

By making pious considerations and holy
affections; these will naturally give rise to good
resolutions; the mind perceives what is good,
the heart feels drawn thereto, and finally the
will, aided by grace, decides on doing it.

**92. Is it useful in meditation to devote some
moments exclusively in the resolutions?**

Yes, although the resolutions are substan-
tially implied in the considerations and affections, and may have been determined already
in the course of the meditation, at least in a

general way, still it is useful and even necessary to devote some moments exclusively to the resolutions, in order to give them more force and precision.

93. Are the resolutions not the effect also of grace?

Undoubtedly, since it is God who works in us not only the good thoughts and pious affections, but also "to will and to accomplish, according to *his* good will." (*Phil.* 2:13). In order to make good resolutions, we must, therefore, multiply and fervently renew our invocations to God, to Our Lord, to the Blessed Virgin, and to our Guardian Angel.

94. Must we make the resolutions which we sometimes find pointed out in meditation books?

No, this is not necessary: for such resolutions may not always prove to be the most useful to us in our actual condition.

95. What qualities should our resolutions have in order to be really profitable?

In order to be really profitable, our resolutions should be:

1. Precise, not vague or general.
2. Practical, not theoretical.

3. Personal, i.e., relating to our duties, our wants, our inclinations, and especially to our predominant passion.

4. Proximate, not for the distant future.

5. Firm.

6. Persevering, i.e., constantly renewed until a satisfactory result is obtained.

96. Finally, to what general end should all our good resolutions be directed?

They should be directed to the accomplishment of God's holy will. It is in conforming our will to His adorable will that we can attain true wisdom, perfection, and happiness.

§ 5. THE ORDER AND CONNECTION OF THESE ACTS

97. In what order are the considerations, affections, and resolutions produced?

Ordinarily the order is the following: considerations, affections, resolutions.

98. Must we always strictly adhere to this order?

No, for sometimes the affections present themselves before the considerations, and the resolutions before the affections; in such cases we must follow the movements or inspirations of divine grace.

99. What important observation can be made on this point?

The observation that in mental prayer the considerations, affections, and resolutions may either follow one another, or intermingle in various ways. The soul in its interview with God must be allowed to act with perfect liberty and simplicity. It should dwell on each of the different parts of mental prayer as long as it feels itself so inclined—now dwelling longer on the considerations, now insisting more on holy affections, now devoting more time to practical resolutions. All this depends on the movements of grace and on the dispositions which animate the soul at the moment.

100. What different names are given to mental prayer according to the predominance of the considerations, the affections, or the resolutions?

Mental prayer is called prayer of meditation when the considerations predominate; it is called affective prayer or prayer of supplication when the affections predominate; it is called prayer of conformity with God's holy will when the resolutions predominate.

CHAPTER IV

CONCLUSION OF MENTAL PRAYER

101. What is meant by the conclusion of mental prayer?

By the conclusion of mental prayer is meant the acts made before retiring from the divine audience.

102. What are these acts?

They are:

1. An act of thanksgiving for the favors obtained during mental prayer.

2. An act of regret for the faults committed during mental prayer.

3. Renewal of the firm purpose to avoid sin and practice virtue.

4. The spiritual bouquet.

5. The colloquy.

6. The concluding vocal prayers.

103. What must we do if we have not yet determined our resolution?

We must determine it at once, according to the indications already given.

104. What is meant by the spiritual bouquet?

By the spiritual bouquet is meant a thought of faith or a maxim taken from the Scriptures or from a saint, a supplication which sums up and recalls to mind the good sentiments and the resolutions of the meditation. We should recall the spiritual bouquet often during the day.

105. What is meant by the colloquy?

By the colloquy is meant a parting word addressed to God, to the Blessed Virgin, or to some saint, on the subject and the purpose of the meditation.

106. Why is mental prayer terminated by some vocal prayers?

In order to recommend to God, to Mary, and to our other heavenly protectors the resolutions and fruits of this exercise.

107. Against what must we be on our guard after meditation?

After meditation we must be on our guard especially against infractions of the rule of silence and against dissipation.

CHAPTER V

EXAMINATION OF MENTAL PRAYER

108. Is it important to examine ourselves on the practice of mental prayer?

Yes, if we wish to advance in this holy exercise.

109. On what points ought the examination to bear?

The examination ought to bear on all the parts of mental prayer: on the preparation, the considerations, the affections, the resolutions, and particularly on the principal resolution; it is useful to look for the predominant defect of our meditations and for the causes thereof.

110. Must we examine ourselves every time on all the above-mentioned points?

No, we should examine ourselves sometimes on one, sometimes on another; the essential thing is to make a short examination every day, and a more complete one on certain days, as on Sundays, but especially on days of retreat.

111. When is the daily examination of mental prayer to be made?

It is to be made immediately after the meditation, or at any other moment of the day, preferably at the particular examen.

112. What would be advisable if we should have to reproach ourselves for some negligence in meditation?

In this case it would be advisable to impose a penance on ourselves, and to compensate for our negligence by making a supplementary meditation of a few minutes during some free moments.

113. What other means may be employed in order to succeed in making mental prayer well?

Keeping an account of it, and submitting it regularly to our spiritual director.

CHAPTER VI

MIXED MENTAL PRAYER

114. What is meant by mixed mental prayer?

By mixed mental prayer is meant mental prayer combined with some other spiritual exercise, as with vocal prayers, spiritual reading, Benediction of the Blessed Sacrament, the Way of the Cross, the assistance at an instruction or conference, Holy Mass, preparation for Holy Communion, etc.

115. Mention some vocal prayers that may easily combine with mental prayer.

The Our Father, the Hail Mary, the Apostles' Creed, the Rosary, the Acts of Faith, Hope, Charity, and Contrition, the Mass prayers, etc.

116. Mention some spiritual books that may furnish matter for mixed mental prayer.

The Holy Scriptures, especially the *Psalms* and the *Gospels,* the *Imitation of Christ,* the *Spiritual Combat,* etc.

117. How then is mixed mental prayer to be made?

1. The ordinary acts of the immediate preparation are made.

2. The subject of the meditation is read or recited slowly, entirely or partially, according to the subject chosen.

3. One point or idea after another is taken up.

4. On each point the considerations, affections and resolutions are made according to the method indicated for the ordinary meditation.

118. Is this kind of mental prayer recommended?

It is earnestly recommended by St. Francis de Sales, St. Alphonsus Liguori, St. Philip Neri, and, in general, by the masters of the spiritual life.

119. When is it advisable to adopt this kind of mental prayer?

When in the exercise of pure mental prayer we meet with difficulties against which we have vainly endeavored to struggle.

120. Against what danger must we be on our guard in the exercise of mixed mental prayer?

Against the danger of changing the meditation into a continued reading or into a mere empty recitation.

121. How may assistance at Benediction of the Blessed Sacrament be combined with mental prayer?

This may be done by using as subjects the liturgical chants and prayers referring to the Blessed Sacrament, some chapter of the fourth book of the *Imitation of Christ,* or one of the *Visits to the Blessed Sacrament* of St. Alphonsus Liguori. We must, however, begin by placing ourselves in the presence of God sacramentally exposed on the altar.

122. How may the Way of the Cross be performed by way of meditation?

This may be done easily by reflections and affections on the sufferings of our Savior, since the Way of the Cross is essentially a meditation on the Passion.

123. How may we attend an instruction by way of meditation?

1. By evoking acts of adherence to the word of God which is being taught.

2. By applying it to ourselves.

3. By producing appropriate affections.

4. By forming corresponding resolutions.

124. How may we assist at Holy Mass by way of meditation?

1. By uniting ourselves in mind and heart to Jesus Christ, who is at once Priest and Victim.

2. By meditating on the four ends or purposes for which the Sacrifice is offered, on God's holy presence, on the ceremonies of the Mass, on the Passion of Our Lord which these ceremonies call to mind, or on some prayer of the Mass.

125. How may the preparation for Holy Communion be combined with mental prayer?

By reflecting on the answers to the following questions:

1. "Who is coming to me?"—"What is His object in coming to me?"—"Who am I that I dare to receive Him?"

2. By producing affections that naturally flow from the above-mentioned reflections, such as acts of faith, admiration, humility, contrition, hope, desire, love, etc.

126. What ought we never to omit when making mixed menial prayer?

We ought never to omit the essential acts of the preparation and conclusion.

CHAPTER VII

DIFFICULTIES ENCOUNTERED IN MENTAL PRAYER

§ 1. DISTRACTIONS

127. What difficulties are frequently met with in mental prayer?

Distractions, aridity, and illusions.

128. What is a distraction?

A distraction is a deviation of the soul from the object which ought to occupy its attention.

129. How many kinds of distractions are there?

There are two kinds of distractions: voluntary and involuntary.

130. When are distractions voluntary? Distractions are voluntary:

1. Directly, or in themselves, when we do not endeavor to banish them as soon as we perceive them.

2. Indirectly, or in their causes, when we do not endeavor to remove the causes.

131. What are the chief causes of our distractions?

The chief causes of our distractions are:

1. Satan.

2. A want of preparation for meditation, especially of the habitual preparation.

3. The natural levity of our mind.

4. The multiplicity of our occupations.

132. Can we remove all these causes?

No, we cannot remove them wholly, but we must struggle against them and endeavor to diminish their sad effects.

133. Are there, then, unavoidable distractions?

Yes, there are distractions which are unavoidable; therefore, we should not be surprised at distractions, still less troubled or agitated; it suffices that we turn our mind back to our prayer as soon as we become aware of their presence.

134. Why does Satan endeavor to distract us during mental prayer?

In order to make us lose the profit which he too well knows we derive from this holy exercise, and, if possible, to make us abandon it entirely.

135. When are distractions involuntary?

They are involuntary:

1. When we have not caused them.

2. When we are not aware of them.

3. When, being aware of them, we do not entertain them freely.

136. Are involuntary distractions culpable?

They are neither culpable nor even injurious.

137. How must we act with regard to distractions?

From the very beginning we must make up our mind to meditate well; then, during the meditation, we must drive from our mind every distraction as soon as we perceive it.

138. What means may be employed to banish distractions?

We may:

1. Humble ourselves for these wanderings of our mind, but without becoming troubled.

2. Recall to our mind the presence of God, of the Blessed Virgin and of our Guardian Angel.

3. Gaze at an object capable of fixing our attention, like the tabernacle, a crucifix, a pious picture, etc.

4. Ask God's help by ejaculatory prayers, and calmly endeavor to take up the subject

of meditation again without ever becoming discouraged.

139. And if we were obliged to pass the entire time destined for meditation in this way, would that be a reason for becoming disheartened?

Not in the least; such a meditation, which St. Francis de Sales calls the meditation of patience, would not on that account be less excellent.

140. Why is the meditation of patience good and meritorious?

Because the sincere will to do what is required for meditation is in itself already a good meditation, and insures all the fruits thereof; besides, the greater our efforts to overcome difficulties, the greater our merits.

§ 2. ARIDITY

141. What is aridity?

Aridity is a state in which the soul finds itself unable to produce the acts of meditation, on account of lack of thought and sentiment.

142. How many kinds of aridity are there?

Two: voluntary (or culpable) aridity, and involuntary aridity.

143. What are the ordinary causes of voluntary aridity?

The ordinary causes of voluntary aridity are:
1. Affection for sin.
2. Habitual dissipation of the mind.
3. Immortification of the passions, such as pride, egotism, sensuality, and lack of simplicity.

144. How must we combat voluntary aridity?

We must combat it in its very causes.

145. What must be done when we suffer from involuntary aridity?

Without permitting agitation or discouragement to lay hold of us, we must simply remember God's presence and try to make acts of faith, humility, confidence, and love, but especially acts of humble supplication, which, as we have seen, are always possible.

146. Can aridity, even when prolonged, prevent our meditation from being excellent?

Not at all, the greatest saints have gone through this painful ordeal.

147. What truths should we recall to mind while in the state of aridity?

We should remember:
1. That virtue does not consist in tender

affections, but in serving God with courage.

2. That God tries by aridity more particularly those whom He loves.

3. That aridity is a source of great spiritual profit.

148. Must we, then, never give way to discouragement?

No, discouragement would be dishonorable to God and detrimental to our soul.

§ 3. ILLUSIONS

149. What are illusions?

Illusions are false ideas which Satan endeavors to plant in our mind in order to make us eventually abandon meditation.

150. Mention some illusions.

1. To believe that mental prayer is too difficult, and that we shall never succeed in performing it well.

2. To believe that it is useless to apply ourselves to mental prayer, since we do not make any progress in virtue anyhow.

3. To judge of the value of our meditation by the consolations or good sentiments we experience.

151. Show the falsity of the first illusion.

Mental prayer, as has already been said and proved, is always possible and even easy for those who are animated with a good will.

152. Show the falsity of the second illusion.

Meditation performed with a good will is necessarily attended by progress in virtue, though the progress may not be perceptible from day to day.

153. In order to make plain the falsity of the third illusion, state by what we should judge of the value of our meditations.

We should judge the value of our meditations especially by the firm determination of our will to reform our lives, to be less selfish. to be more charitable, more submissive to God's holy will, more obedient, more pure. and more humble.

154. What benefits accrue to us from the difficulties of meditation?

The difficulties of meditation contribute to maintain us in humility, insure our progress in solid virtue, prevent remissness and illusions, and increase our merits.

SUPPLEMENT

Following are some suggested prayers to enable the beginner to prepare for mental prayer and also to make his thanksgiving and resolution afterwards. When a person is accustomed to the practice of mental prayer, these can be replaced by prayers said extemporaneously from the heart, but the general format of a) *preparation*, b) *body*, and c) *conclusion* should always remain.

§ ACTS OF THE PREPARATION

Invocation of the Holy Ghost

Come, Holy Ghost, have compassion on my poverty, in order that, illuminated, moved, and guided by Thee, I may make my prayer well. Come, enlighten my intellect, inflame my heart, and convert my will, that my prayer may contribute to Thy glory and to my own spiritual advancement.

Invocation of the Blessed Virgin

O Mary, my good and tender Mother, thou who didst continually ponder in thy heart the

words of Jesus, thou whose life was uninter-
rupted prayer, assist me in acquitting myself
of this holy exercise in conformity with thy
desire and with that of thy Divine Son.

Invocation of the Guardian Angel

Angel Guardian, thou who beholdest unceasingly the countenance of the Lord, thou
who always standest in His holy presence, faith
teaches me that thou art given to me as my
light, my guide, and my helper; assist me,
therefore, in the interview that I am about to
have with my God.

Act of Faith in the Presence of God

O my God, I firmly believe that Thou art
here present. Thou dost penetrate my whole
being. I am before Thee as if I were alone in
this world. Thou dost see me, hear me, and
know my most secret thoughts.

(If the meditation is made before the Blessed Sacrament, the following act is to be added.)

O my God, I believe that Thou art really
present in the Most Holy Sacrament, and that
Thou dost actually direct toward me from Thy
tabernacle the same regard of tenderness
which Thou didst so mercifully cast upon Thy

disciples, and even upon sinners, during Thy mortal life.

Act of Adoration

Prostrate before Thy Infinite Majesty, I adore Thee, O my God, as my Creator and the sovereign Lord of all things. I acknowledge with delight Thy supreme dominion over me and all creatures. Glory, honor, love, and submission be to Thee, the King of Heaven, at all times and in all places! During this audience I unite my adoration and homage with those of Our Lord Jesus Christ, of the Blessed Virgin, of the whole heavenly court, of the souls in Purgatory, of all the faithful upon earth, and in particular with those of the persons here present.

(If the meditation is made before the Blessed Sacrament, the following act is to be added.)

I adore Thee, O Jesus, present in the Holy Eucharist. I acknowledge Thee as my Savior and sovereign Lord. In union with the angels and saints surrounding Thy throne of mercy, I exclaim: "Praise and adoration be forever to Jesus in the Most Holy Sacrament!"

Act of Humility

But who am I, O my God, that I dare to

appear before Thee? Thou art All and I am but nothingness and weakness. I have nothing of my own but my infidelities. Without Thee I cannot so much as conceive a good thought.

Act of Contrition

O Jesus, my Savior, who didst die on the cross to atone for my sins, I deplore my waywardness in the bitterness of my soul. Have mercy on me and pardon my ingratitude; deign to apply to my soul the merits of Thy holy Passion; grant that I may resolve, in this meditation, never more to relapse into sin, in order that I may obtain mercy on the day of judgment.

Act of Thanksgiving

I thank Thee, O my God, for all the graces and benefits Thou hast bestowed on me to this day. I thank Thee particularly for my vocation, and for the singular favor Thou dost presently grant me in admitting me to this celestial audience.

Act of Confidence

O my God, Thou didst command me to call Thee by the sweet name of Father; I come, therefore, O Father, to ask of Thee, with the most childlike confidence, whatever is necessary to converse worthily with Thee during this meditation. Captivate my attention, enlighten my understanding, inflame my heart, direct and strengthen my will, that I may lose none of the fruits Thou dost intend to bestow upon me during this holy exercise.

Act of Union with Our Lord

O my Savior, I wish to perform this holy exercise with the intentions and dispositions Thou didst have when praying to Thy heavenly Father during Thy mortal life, and which Thou hast now while praying in our tabernacles. Thou art our spiritual Head, and I am a member of Thy Mystical Body. Meditate, I beseech Thee, through this member, however unworthy it be; ask of Thy heavenly Father, through me and for me, whatever is at this moment most necessary and useful for my soul. Amen.

§ ACTS OF THE BODY OF MENTAL PRAYER

Here one should make his a) *Considerations* (See especially Questions 67-75), b) *Affections* (See especially Questions 76-86), and c) *Resolutions* (See especially Questions 89-96).

§ ACTS OF THE CONCLUSION

Act of Thanksgiving

O my God, I thank Thee for the audience with which Thou hast honored me. I thank Thee for all the inspirations and good senti-ments Thou hast imparted to me, and for all the good resolutions Thou hast suggested to me.

Act of Regret

O my God, I ask Thy pardon for all the neg-ligences of which I have made myself guilty during this holy exercise. I profoundly hum-ble myself for them. Have mercy on me, O my God, and do not permit that my care-lessness may deprive me of the graces Thy goodness had prepared for me.

Renewal of the Resolution

O my God, I renew with more determina-tion than ever the resolution to . . . and in order to be faithful to it, I will adopt the fol-lowing means . . .

Spiritual Bouquet

For my spiritual bouquet I shall take these words . . . I will often repeat them during the day and especially on this or that occasion . . .

Colloquy

O my God, bless again this resolution before I withdraw, that I may always remain faithful to it. Dearest Virgin Mary, my good and tender Mother, into thy hands I deposit the fruits of this meditation, as also all my other spiritual goods. Preserve and increase them, that thy child may become less unworthy of thee. St. N . . . , obtain for me the grace to be faithful to my resolution. Dear Guardian Angel, remove far from me every cause of dissipation, which would expose me to lose the fruits of my meditation.

Vocal Prayer

(Here one should conclude the exercise of mental prayer with vocal prayers of his own choice, recommending further to God, to Mary, and to his other heavenly protectors the resolutions and fruits of this exercise.)

A CHOICE OF SUBJECTS FOR MEDITATION

1. The doctrines on mental prayer as contained in this book.

2. The ordinary prayers of a Christian: and among these, principally the Our Father, the Hail Mary, and, above all, the Apostles' Creed.

3. The hymn *Veni Creator,* the prose *Veni Sancte Spiritus,* and the invocation *Veni Swale Spiritus!* (Come, Holy Ghost!).

4. The Acts of Faith, Hope, Charity, Contrition, oblation, adoration, thanksgiving, etc., and the doxology (Glory Be to the Father . . .).

5. The acts before and after Communion.

6. The Mass prayers.

7. The mysteries of our holy religion, particularly the mysteries of the Holy Rosary, the other mysteries of the life of our Savior, of the Blessed Virgin, of the saints, and above all, the Passion, the Holy Eucharist, and the Sacred Heart.

8. The Litany of the Holy Name of Jesus.

9. The Litany of the Blessed Virgin, the *Ave Maris Stella,* the *Magnificat,* the *Salve Regina,* the *Memorare,* the *Sub Tuum,* and the antiphons

in honor of the Immaculate Conception.

10. The Litany of the Saints, particularly the invocations which terminate it.

11. Holy Writ, particularly the Psalms and the Biblical narratives, the Sermon on the Mount (*Matt.* 5:3-12), Our Lord's discourse after the Last Supper (*John* 13-17), and the parables, such as those of the Prodigal Son (*Luke* 15:11-32) and of the Pharisee and the Publican. (*Luke* 18:9-14).

12. *The Following of Christ, The Spiritual Combat,* the writings of St. Alphonsus Liguori, etc.

13. For priests, the ordination prayers in the *Manual of Ordinations.*

14. For religious, the formula of their religious profession, and their Rule.

15. For all, the prayers of the Ritual for the administration of Baptism, Confirmation, Extreme Unction, and the prayers for the agonizing; finally, the prayers for the dead, and the Office of the Dead.

A CHOICE OF SPIRITUAL BOUQUETS

It will be noticed at a glance that the following aspirations and texts may at the same time be used as subjects of meditation. Fatigued or distracted minds will find them to be a delightful spiritual symposium, if only they will take the trouble of perusing them.

1. O Sacrament most holy! O Sacrament divine!

   All praise and all thanksgiving be every moment Thine!

2. O sweetest Heart of Jesus, I implore that I may ever love Thee more and more!

3. Jesus, meek and humble of heart, make my heart like unto Thine!

4. Sweet Heart of Jesus, be my love!

5. My Jesus, mercy!

6. Jesus, Mary and Joseph, I give thee my heart and my soul!

   Jesus, Mary and Joseph, assist me in my last agony!

   Jesus, Mary and Joseph, may I breathe forth my soul in peace with thee!

7. Sweet Heart of Mary, be my salvation!

8. My Queen, my Mother, remember I am thine own; keep me, guard me as thy property and thy possession.

9. Angel of God, my guardian dear,
To whom God's love commits me here,
Ever this day be at my side,
To light and guard, to rule and guide!

10. O Mary, conceived without sin, pray for us who have recourse to thee!

11. Immaculate Heart of Mary, pray for us!

12. Praised be Jesus, now and forever! Amen.

13. May the Sacred Heart of Jesus be loved in every place!

14. Jesus, my God, I love Thee above all things!

15. My God and my All!

16. All for the greater honor and glory of God!

17. My sweetest Jesus, be not my Judge but my Savior!

18. All for Jesus!

19. Eternal rest grant unto them, O Lord, and let perpetual light shine upon them!

20. O Lord, Thou knowest that I love Thee!

21. O Lord, teach us how to pray!

22. Lord, that I may see.

23. Thy will be done!

24. Lord, I am not worthy that Thou shouldst enter under my roof.

25. Put ye on the Lord Jesus Christ.

26. My meat is to do the will of Him Who sent me.

27. Lord, that I may know Thee, that I may know myself!

28. Give us this day our daily bread.

29. Lord, increase our faith.

30. Faith removes mountains!

31. My delight is to be with the children of men.

32. Love one another as I have loved you.

33. Behold thy Mother!

34. Be ye perfect as your heavenly Father is perfect.

35. He that hopeth in the Lord shall not be confounded.

36. If God is for us, who can be against us?

37. Father, forgive them, for they know not what they do.

38. Blessed are the meek, for they shall possess the land.

39. The Lord hath given and the Lord hath taken away. Blessed be the name of the Lord!

40. Through many tribulations we must enter into the kingdom of God.

41. Behold, now is the acceptable time!
42. I am the Good Shepherd.
43. He was subject to them.
44. Go to Joseph!
45. Remember, man, that thou art dust, and unto dust thou shalt return.
46. Judge not, that you may not be judged.
47. Obedience is the tomb of self-will.
48. Speak, Lord, for Thy servant heareth.
49. My son, give Me thy heart.
50. Blessed are the clean of heart, for they shall see God.
51. Whether you eat or drink, or whatsoever else you do, do all to the glory of God.
52. My grace is sufficient for thee.
53. The crown is given to him who fights.
54. In the sweat of thy brow shalt thou eat bread.
55. God loveth a cheerful giver.
56. The life of man upon earth is a war-fare.
57. If thou didst know the gift of God!
58. If any man will come after Me, let him deny himself.
59. He was wounded for our iniquities, He was bruised for our sins.
60. Without Me you can do nothing.
61. In all thy works remember thy last end, and thou shalt never sin.

62. Time is worth as much as God.

63. Unless you do penance, you shall likewise perish.

64. The obedient man shall speak of victory.

65. He that contemneth small things shall fall by little and little.

66. The tongue is a world of iniquity.

67. God resisteth the proud, but to the humble He giveth grace.

68. Remove self-will, and there will be no Hell.

69. Whom the Lord loveth He chastiseth.

70. Of what use will this be for my eternity?

71. I was born for greater things.

72. Bernard, why hast thou come hither?

73. Our conversation is in Heaven.

74. Serve ye the Lord with gladness.

75. Watch and pray.

76. What doth it profit a man if he gain the whole world and suffer the loss of his own soul?

77. Come to Me, all ye who labor and are burdened, and I will refresh you.

78. My yoke is sweet and My burden light.

79. Keep the Rule and the Rule will keep you.

80. Idleness hath taught much evil.

81. Prayer is the key to Heaven.

82. He who prays well, lives well.

83. Father, I have sinned against Heaven and before Thee; I am not now worthy to be called Thy son.

84. Every idle word that men shall speak, they shall render an account for it in the day of judgment.

85. Knowledge puffeth up.

86. The kingdom of Heaven suffereth violence.

87. Hedge in thy ears with thorns, and hear not a wicked tongue.

88. They that are Christ's have crucified their flesh with its vices and concupiscences.

89. Pride is hateful before God and men.

90. The world is crucified to me and I to the world.

91. Humility is the mother and guardian of all virtues.

92. Everyone that exalteth himself shall be humbled, and he that humbleth himself shall be exalted.

93. Obedience is better than sacrifice.

94. He that heareth you heareth Me, and he that despiseth you despiseth Me.

95. The fear of the Lord is the beginning of wisdom.

96. I am the Way, and the Truth, and the Life.

97. As long as you did it to one of these My least brethren, you did it to Me.

98. Do good to them that hate you, and pray for them that persecute and calumniate you.

99. The north wind driveth away rain, as doth a sad countenance a backbiting tongue.

100. A servant of Mary shall not perish.

QUESTIONS FOR THE EXAMINATION OF MENTAL PRAYER

The following questions are intended for the daily examination.

Remote Preparation. Was I watchful over my senses yesterday?—Was I interiorly recollected?—Did I keep silence?—Did I observe modesty?—Did I avoid sin and the occasions of sin?—Did I recite ejaculatory prayers?—Did I make my spiritual exercises conscientiously?

Proximate Preparation. Did I choose a subject for meditation?—Did I recall it while retiring and again after rising?—Was I attentive during the reading of the subject?

Immediate Preparation. Did I, and how did I, perform the acts of the immediate preparation?—the act of faith?—the act of adoration?—the act of humility?—the act of petition?—Was I penetrated with the thought of the presence of God?

Considerations. Did I apply myself seriously to them?—Did I make them in the light of faith?—Did I make the application to myself?

Affections. Did I make many and fervent affections?

Resolutions. Did I observe the resolution of my last meditation?—If not, what was the cause of my unfaithfulness?—Was my resolution precise, practical, and firm?

Conclusion. Did I, and *how* did I, perform the act of thanksgiving?—the act of contrition?—Did I choose a spiritual bouquet?—Did I give some attention to the colloquy?

Various Difficulties. Did I give way to discouragement on account of the wanderings of my mind and the hardness of my heart, instead of humbling myself, arming myself with patience, confidently having recourse to God and the Most Holy Virgin, and endeavoring to continue my meditation, if necessary, with the aid of a book?—Were not dissipation and faults against silence the cause of my distractions in meditation?—Did I experience aridity?—Was it not caused by venial sins deliberately committed?—by natural and disorderly affections?—by immortification and infidelities to the Rule?—After I found out the culpable causes of the faults committed during meditation, did I impose a penance upon myself?—If I was drowsy, did I take means to overcome drowsiness?

Did I make the account of the last meditation?

PRACTICAL REMARKS

1. Never make of your meditation a mere spiritual reading, still less a study. The meditation is essentially a conversation with God.

2. Never neglect, on whatever subject you meditate, to make suitable applications to yourself.

3. If the meditation is preceded by a reading, the considerations need not take up much time because they are supposed to have been made already, to some extent at least, during the reading; if that was the case, apply yourself almost immediately to the affections, or, better still, make the considerations in the form of affections.

4. Always give a very large place to the affections. The affections really make of the meditation a mental prayer. Affections of faith, petition, humility, thanksgiving, and love should find a place in every meditation.

5. Make all the resolutions that are suggested by the considerations and affections in the course of the meditation. But toward the end of the meditation, select from among the many, one special resolution, which shall be

the resolution properly so called, and give it all the required qualifications.

6. As much as possible, make your meditation in the form of a colloquy (*to*, rather than *about*, God and Our Lady). Habitually keep your eyes on the tabernacle and converse familiarly and lovingly with Him who is present therein on purpose for you. Although the entire meditation, even the considerations and resolutions, be made in the form of a colloquy, there should, however, be among the acts of the conclusion, a final colloquy, or the colloquy properly so called, which consists in offering up to God, or to the Blessed Virgin, or to some saint, the resolution for the coming day, and in begging earnestly for the grace of being faithful to it.

7. No one special method is obligatory for meditation. Thus it is not necessary to make all the acts in every meditation, nor to make them in their natural order, namely, the considerations first, then the affections, and finally the resolutions. Be perfectly free in this respect. Consult your dispositions, your needs, the inspirations of grace and the nature of the subject you are meditating upon, and do not adhere too strictly to the method; the method is meant to be a help, not a hindrance.

8. Always aim at what is practical. Be practical in making the considerations by applying to yourself what you are considering; theoretical considerations, however good in themselves, fall short of spiritual profit, unless they are made to enter the sphere of practical life. Be practical in making the affections by giving the preference to such affections as are more in harmony with the state of your soul. Be practical, above all, in the choice of resolutions, because principally upon the resolutions rests the task of realizing the usefulness of meditation.

9. When, through serious indisposition of mind or body, you find yourself incapable of applying yourself to regular meditation, you may rest satisfied with reviewing beforehand the different duties in which you are to be employed during the day, considering how you can best fulfill them in a manner pleasing to God and edifying to others. You may also complain to God, as you would to your spiritual director, of your inability to meditate, of your miseries, which you may enumerate, and of your many failures in the practice of virtue, thus humbling yourself and realizing your own nothingness. If your inability to meditate is so great that you cannot do

even this, then at least look respectfully toward the tabernacle and keep on saying in your heart with a sincere conviction of your littleness and a deep sentiment of humility: "My Jesus, mercy!" or some other short aspiration. If you do this you shall have made a good meditation.

A FINAL REMINDER

1. Remember that meditation is the "art of becoming better." Everything must be directed to this end: preparations, considerations, applications, affections, resolutions. If meditation is not considered from this standpoint, it will be impossible to understand why the ascetic writers are so enthusiastic over this exercise, why all religious founders have given it such a prominent place in their Rules, and why all good religious are scrupulously in earnest about its performance.

2. Remember that meditation is a kind of daily retreat. As during the annual retreat you examine and set aright what was amiss in the preceding year, and provide yourself with good purposes for the coming year as on the day of the monthly retreat you throw one glance back upon the past month and another forward into the coming month; in like manner, in your daily meditation, you look back upon the past day in order to see how you spent it, and you look forward into the present day in order to see how you can make the best use of it for the glory of God and the welfare of your soul.

3. Remember that to make a good meditation only one thing is necessary; good will. Sublime views, nice expressions, learning, even correct language, are not necessary. On the other hand, distractions, aridity, drowsiness, fatigue, and even disgust, are no hindrance to a good meditation when there is GOOD WILL.